EUROPE

ASIA

Mediterranean Sea

AFRICA

th China Sea

AUSTRALIA

the world of the

PIRATE

the world of the PIRATE

Val Garwood

Illustrations by
Richard Berridge

PETER BEDRICK BOOKS
NEW YORK

Author's dedication
For Rosa and Dan

Published by
PETER BEDRICK BOOKS
156 Fifth Avenue
New York, NY 10010

Text and illustrations © 1997 Macdonald Young Books, an imprint of Wayland Publishers Limited

Published by agreement with Macdonald Young Books, U.K.

Commissioning editor: Hazel Songhurst
Editor: Ruth Thomson
Designer: Edward Kinsey
Consultant: Simon Stephens,
Curator of Ships,
National Maritime Museum,
Greenwich, UK.

Library of Congress
Cataloging-in-Publication Data
Garwood, Val.
    The World of the pirate / Val Garwood;
illustrations by Richard Berridge.
    p.   cm.
    Included index.
Summary: Relates the history of sea robbers
who plundered ships' cargoes since ancient
times, who flourished in the New World, and
who remain active today, mainly in the South
China Seas.
    ISBN 0-87226-281-2
1. Pirates--Juvenile literature. [1. Pirates.] I.
Berridge, Richard, ill. II. Title.
G535.G35 1997
910.4'5--DC21
                                97–18133
                                CIP
                                AC

Printed in Portugal
Second Printing, 1998

 **AL GARWOOD**

Val Garwood is an Education Officer at the National Maritime Museum in Greenwich, London. She previously worked as a primary school teacher. She has an M.A. in History from the University of London.

 ICHARD BERRIDGE

Since graduating from art college in 1970, the illustrator Richard Berridge has specialized in historical, figurative art. His work reflects his fascination for historical costume and detail and what he describes as the 'theatricality' of the past.

CONTENTS

6..... Introduction

8 ..... Early Sea Robbers

10 ..... Corsairs

12 ..... The Spanish Main

14 ..... The Indian Ocean

16 ..... Privateers

18 ..... Buccaneers

20 ..... Ships

22 ..... Inside a Ship

24 ..... Navigation

26 ..... Work on Board

28 ..... Clothes

30 ..... Life on Board

32 ..... Discipline

34 ..... Illness and Injury

36 ..... Treasure

38 ..... Weapons

40 ..... Attack

42 ..... Pirates Defeated

44 ..... Pirates on Trial

46 ..... Who's Who

48 ..... Index

$\mathcal{I}$NTRODUCTION

Pirates! The word instantly conjures up vivid images of swashbuckling adventurers, brandishing terrifying weapons as they swoop upon chests overflowing with gold and silver treasure. But, in reality, were pirates and their world like this? Were they brave and daring, or violent and cruel, and were their lives as exciting and glamorous as they seem in fiction?

Pirates are water-borne robbers. From ancient times, they have roamed oceans, seas and rivers, violently plundering ships' cargoes. In the fourth century BC pirates even threatened the ships of the powerful emperor, Alexander the Great. In the 1200s, the explorer, Marco Polo, described the dangers of encountering a pirate ship.

After Spanish explorers established regular contact with the Americas in the 1500s, piracy flourished in the New World. Any vessel, from heavy galleons laden with fantastic riches bound for Spain to local fishing boats, was a potential target. Until the 1720s, the exploits of the pirates were so successful that the time was considered the 'Golden Age' of piracy. Even today, piracy continues, although it is mainly confined to the South China Seas.

People did not become pirates because they were especially violent and cruel. Many were already hardened sailors from navies of various countries who turned to piracy when the end of a war made them unemployed. Some had served on merchant ships and were lured by tales of fortunes to be made, while others had run away from slavery or work as servants. Life on board any sailing ship was hard and often brutal, but life on board a pirate ship offered greater freedom and democracy. Crew members could help make the rules by which a pirate ship operated and elect their own captain.

Pirates were usually realistic about whom they attacked, avoiding targets that could not be captured easily. Frequently, victims were so terrified by the mere sight and sound of pirates that their ships were seized with little fighting. Macabre banners, with more varied designs than the Jolly Roger usually flown in fiction, added to the pirates' fearsome reputation.

Precious cargoes of glittering treasure were sometimes seized, but real pirates also stole practical objects. Anything that could be easily resold was considered a worthwhile prize. Although fascinating tales of treasure maps and buried chests abound, these grew from popular stories woven wholly around fictional pirates.

The most famous pirate characters are those who left enough evidence for some of their bold ventures to be recounted. Since it was against their interests to leave evidence of their illegal activities, the great majority of pirates have left no trace behind.

In the 1700s, governments took strong measures to combat piracy. After relentless pursuit, some of the most awesome pirates fell in gory battles. Others were executed with great publicity, but most shared the more mundane fate of ordinary sailors, becoming victim of diseases, accidents and shipwrecks.

After the numbers of pirates operating in the Americas dropped from its peak in the 1720s, fear of them also lessened. Myths about the lives of the 'Golden Age' pirates then took hold. These sea-going robbers gained a romantic appeal never felt for similar criminals on dry land, and heroic stories of their adventures overshadowed the reality of their hard lives and grisly deaths.

EARLY SEA ROBBERS

At the time of the ancient Greeks and Romans, piracy mainly took place on the Aegean and Mediterranean seas. Heavily laden, slow moving trading ships were tempting targets for water borne marauders with swift oared galleys. The sailors followed unvarying trade routes and always kept land in sight, fearful that if they strayed into uncharted waters they would be lost forever. This gave sea robbers an enormous advantage, because it meant that the movements of their victims were completely predictable. Eventually, both Greek and Roman empires developed strong navies to stop the sea robbers from raiding so successfully. Not all sea robbers carried out attacks at sea. The Vikings, skilled sailors from Denmark, Sweden and Norway, used their fast longships to mount terrifying surprise attacks upon both coastal and inland settlements of northern Europe.

THE GREEK GALLEY

In a galley like this, Greek pirates bore down upon a merchant ship and, with terrific force, aimed its sharp ram into the side. Phoenician ships carrying amber or silver were their favorite targets.

THE ROMANS

Roman merchant ships carried vital food and supplies between different parts of their vast empire. They too were the target of ruthless pirates using speedy galleys, often launched from the coast of North Africa. These sea robbers caused such disruption that powerful war galleys, each with several banks of rowers, were sent from Rome to try to stop them.

Olive oil and wine were cargoes highly valued by pirates. They were transported from Rome to Britain in clay jars called amphorae. The long shape of these amphorae meant that many could be packed tightly together in the limited space of a ship's hold.

amphorae

Grain was one of the most attractive cargoes for sea robbers, because it was so easy to sell. Rome was dependent upon imported grain grown in Egypt, so the constant robberies caused food shortages.

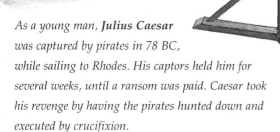

*As a young man, **Julius Caesar** was captured by pirates in 78 BC, while sailing to Rhodes. His captors held him for several weeks, until a ransom was paid. Caesar took his revenge by having the pirates hunted down and executed by crucifixion.*

Catapults were used on board ship as well as on land. When the twisted sinew that acted as a spring was released, the force hurled arrows or large stones at the enemy. The power of a stone missile was sometimes strong enough to decapitate someone.

THE VIKINGS

Viking seafarers from Scandinavia launched countless daring raids. From the end of the 8th century, these attacks continued for more than three centuries. Vikings plundered on both land and sea. The sight of their approaching longships struck terror into the hearts of people, for these sea robbers came in search of slaves as well as rich booty.

A Viking longship was both light and fast. Its shallow hull enabled it to travel a long way up rivers and come in close to shore. Sailors believed that the dragon at the front would bring them luck and scare their enemies. The open ships were too exposed to be used in cold weather, so raids began in the spring. The crew ate cold dried meat or salted fish as it was too dangerous to light a fire on a wooden ship.

FACT AND FICTION
⚓

Viking longships are sometimes shown with a row of shields slung over the side. In fact, the shields were far too precious to be risked in this way and were hung like this only when a longship was in port.

⚓

Viking helmets never had horns. Most warriors fought in close-fitting leather caps rather than helmets. Helmets were extremely expensive and worn only by high-ranking Vikings.

Anglo-Saxon villages and monasteries were frequent Viking targets. Young and healthy villagers were forced on to the longships and transported back to Scandinavia.. There, they were sold in markets as slaves to work on farms. Monasteries offered rich pickings, such as illuminated books, gold and silver cups and crosses. The monks were poor at fighting and offered little resistance to the onslaught of these fierce raiders.

A Viking warrior fought with axe, sword and spear. His iron sword, his most important possession, had a double-edged blade and a leather-covered handle for good grip. His strong shield was made of wooden boards, either covered in leather or painted. The metal boss in the center protected the warrior's hand.

CORSAIRS

Christian and Muslim corsairs were professional fighters who roamed the Mediterranean for hundreds of years, raiding foreign merchant ships to capture their crews for slaves. Christian corsairs were based in Malta. Most Muslim corsairs, including the famous Barbarossa brothers, operated from three large ports along the Barbary coast of North Africa, whose rulers issued licenses granting them permission to operate. By the 1700s, when France, Holland and England had built up strong navies, their threats of retaliation against the corsairs gained their ships safe passage. Weaker countries had to pay the corsairs if they wanted their vessels to trade. Mounting demands for huge sums of protection and ransom money led to war between the United States and Tripoli in 1801, during which Stephen Decatur led a daring raid to destroy a captured US ship, the *Philadelphia*. A peace treaty ended the payments to Tripoli, but those to other Barbary states did not stop until 1816.

THE BARBAROSSA BROTHERS

Aruj and Kheir-ed-Din, known as the Barbarossa ('red-beard') brothers, built the Barbary ports into strong bases. With their fleet of galleys, they captured ships from Spain and Italy as well as treasure ships belonging to Pope Julius II. In 1518, the elder brother, Aruj, fell in battle against the Spanish. Kheir-ed-Din controlled the city of Algiers until his death in 1546.

The main Barbary ports were Tripoli, Algiers and Tunis. They were heavily fortified, with high walls, fortresses and hundreds of cannon. From the 1500s, corsair attacks from these ports into the Mediterranean increased. Corsairs from Algiers sometimes ventured into the Atlantic to plunder ships.

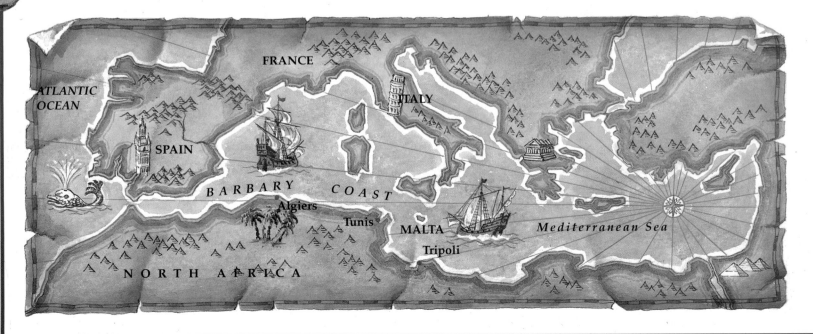

ATLANTIC OCEAN · SPAIN · FRANCE · ITALY · BARBARY COAST · Algiers · Tunis · MALTA · Tripoli · Mediterranean Sea · NORTH AFRICA

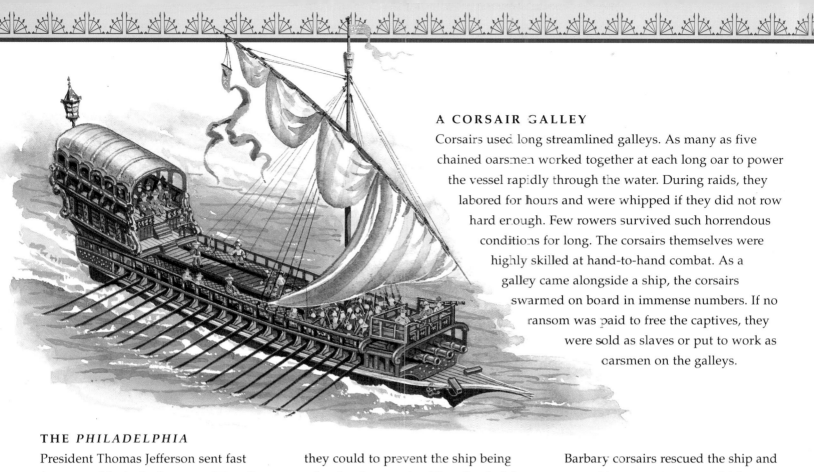

A CORSAIR GALLEY

Corsairs used long streamlined galleys. As many as five chained oarsmen worked together at each long oar to power the vessel rapidly through the water. During raids, they labored for hours and were whipped if they did not row hard enough. Few rowers survived such horrendous conditions for long. The corsairs themselves were highly skilled at hand-to-hand combat. As a galley came alongside a ship, the corsairs swarmed on board in immense numbers. If no ransom was paid to free the captives, they were sold as slaves or put to work as oarsmen on the galleys.

THE *PHILADELPHIA*

President Thomas Jefferson sent fast frigates to blockade the port of Tripoli. Disaster struck in 1804, when one of these ships, the *Philadelphia*, ran aground while pursuing some corsairs. Before the crew surrendered, they did everything they could to prevent the ship being taken by the corsairs. They flooded the powder store, toppled cannon overboard and drilled holes in the bottom of the ship. Nonetheless, the Barbary corsairs rescued the ship and turned it into a pirate vessel. The captain of the *Philadelphia* and more than 300 of his crew were taken prisoner and jailed.

STEPHEN DECATUR

Using a captured Tripolitan ship, US Lieutenant Decatur led a group, some disguised in Arab clothing, past enemy ships and a heavily armed castle to board the *Philadelphia*. They set the ship alight with gunpowder and sailed to safety. The following year, Tripoli agreed to allow American ships safe passage in future and America paid $60,000 for the release of the captured crew.

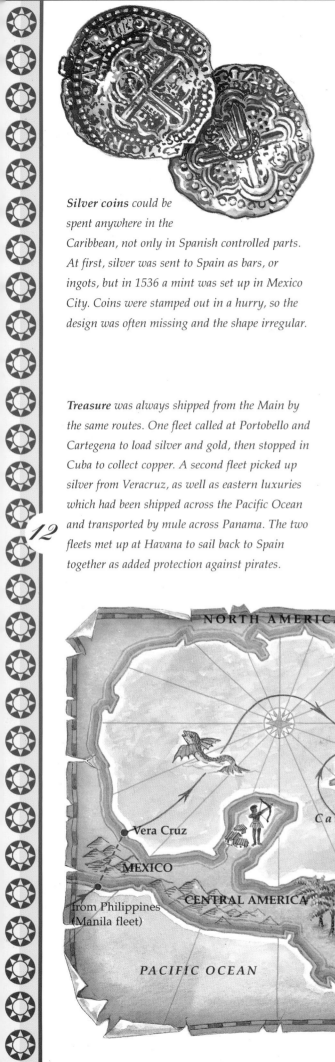

Silver coins could be spent anywhere in the Caribbean, not only in Spanish controlled parts. At first, silver was sent to Spain as bars, or ingots, but in 1536 a mint was set up in Mexico City. Coins were stamped out in a hurry, so the design was often missing and the shape irregular.

Treasure was always shipped from the Main by the same routes. One fleet called at Portobello and Cartegena to load silver and gold, then stopped in Cuba to collect copper. A second fleet picked up silver from Veracruz, as well as eastern luxuries which had been shipped across the Pacific Ocean and transported by mule across Panama. The two fleets met up at Havana to sail back to Spain together as added protection against pirates.

T HE SPANISH MAIN

After Columbus made his exploratory voyage to the Americas in 1492, the Spanish soon discovered areas on the mainland of Central and South America that were fabulously rich in silver, gold and gems. The Pope agreed to grant much of this land to Spain, so it became known as the Spanish Main. This name later included the islands of the Caribbean Sea as well. As Spanish treasure fleets began to cross the Atlantic, news quickly spread of the vast wealth they carried. Since the Spanish forbade inhabitants of their new settlements from trading with other countries, it was not long before pirate raids were mounted on any tempting target, whether ship, port or mule train. The treasure fleets kept to the same shipping lanes in the Atlantic and Caribbean at regular times of year, so it was not difficult for pirates to find them. The pirates made their bases in the most ideal spots for launching attacks. From the Bahamas, they intercepted ships passing through the Florida Straits. Another favorite spot was the Windward Passage between Cuba and Hispaniola. For more than two centuries the Spanish Main became the central area for a 'Golden Age' of piracy.

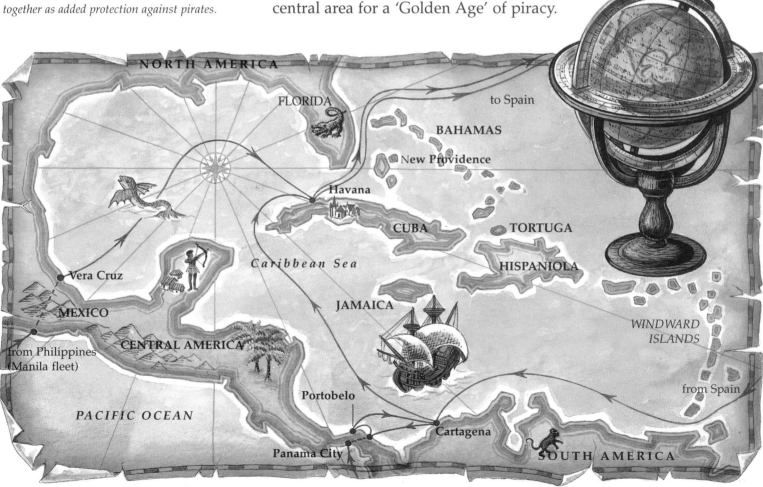

A CARIBBEAN PORT

Once the Spanish realized the extent of the riches to be had in the Americas, they began to build ports and towns there. At first, defenseless coastal towns were vulnerable to ruthless pirate attacks. Finally, the Spanish built strong fortifications to their ports, which made pirate looting much more difficult.

The rich exports of the Spanish Main were loaded into small rowing boats, which ferried them to waiting galleons. It took many trips before all the sacks, chests and barrels were securely loaded into the hold of the ships.

The silver mines at Potosi in Peru were the source of much of the Spanish treasure. Silver ore was dug from inside the mountain and carried downhill by llamas, to be sorted, washed, smelted into bars and minted into coins. Native people were forced to work as slaves in the mines. Huge numbers died because of the horrendous working conditions, and West African slaves were shipped to work in the mines in their places.

13

THE INDIAN OCEAN

Dhows were small fast ships used by Arab pirates. They were rigged with triangular, or lateen, sails which made them speedy and very easy to maneuver.

Pirates who ranged across the Indian Ocean attacked ships loaded with silk, spices and other luxury products of the east, such as fine china. These cargoes had long been the target of Indian and Arab pirates, who had operated in the area since ancient times. For many years, some of the pirates active in the Caribbean had also crossed the Atlantic in search of gold, ivory or slaves from the west coast of Africa. Towards the end of the 1600s, their hunting grounds in the Spanish Main became better defended, so some began to make the long additional journey around the Cape of Good Hope into the Indian Ocean and Red Sea. The victims of pirates such as Henry Avery and Thomas Tew, were the sumptuous treasure fleets of the Indian rulers, the Moghuls, and the large merchant ships of Britain, France and the Dutch East India Company. The pirate booty was often shared out on the island haven of Madagascar.

14

A busy trading network had existed in the Indian Ocean for hundreds of years. Heavily laden ships made use of the prevailing monsoon winds to carry their cargoes between east Africa, Arabia and India.

Cargo ships from the Moluccas, the famed Spice Islands, followed a specific shipping route, which was controlled first by the Portuguese and then by the Dutch, who conquered these islands one after the other.

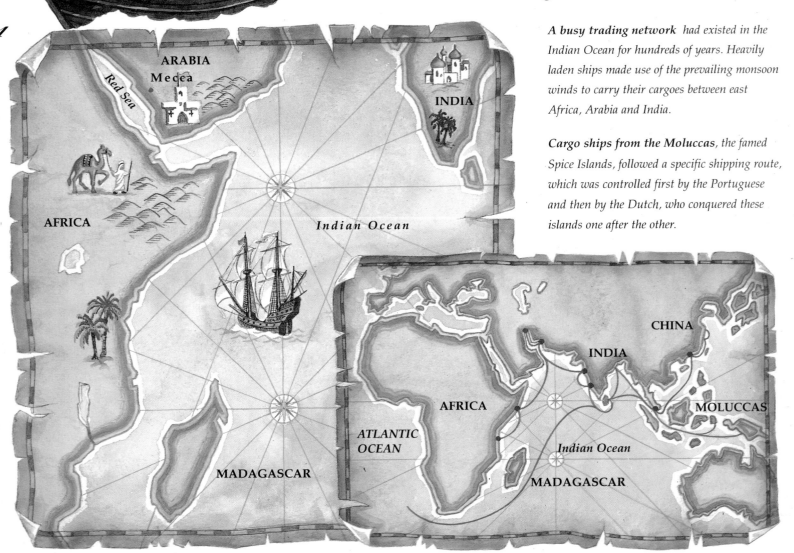

SPICES

Spices were vital for preserving food, especially meat, in the days before refrigeration. They were luxury products, bought cheaply from growers in India and the Spice Islands, and re-sold in Europe at enormous profit. Cargoes of spice took up a lot of space, so some pirates preferred to attack the ships carrying the gold for buying spices, rather than seizing the spice cargoes themselves.

Cloves

Ginger

Silk cloth

Rolls of delicate fabrics, such as silk and muslin, were often beautifully embroidered with gold and silver thread.

Nutmeg

Cinnamon sticks

TEW AND AVERY

Pirates Thomas Tew and Henry Avery mounted profitable attacks in the Indian Ocean working separately and together.

The island of Madagascar was ideally situated for launching attacks and was a perfect pirate base. Sheltered in one of its many secluded bays, pirates could take on board fresh supplies of food and drink, repair their ships and rest after attacks.

Thomas Tew, originally from Rhode Island, made rich profits raiding ships in the Indian Ocean and Red Sea, plundering their cargoes of precious jewels, ivory and silk. He was killed in 1695 on an expedition with Avery, while boarding an Indian trading ship.

Henry Avery's most daring attack was against a large ship, called the Ganj Suwai that belonged to the Grand Moghul of India. It was carrying pilgrims home from Mecca in 1695. Avery's crew used torture to rob the pilgrims of their valuables. The huge treasure haul included half a million coins, which the crew divided between themselves.

A letter of marque was a special licence issued by a monarch or governor giving privateers permission to attack enemy ships. It was issued in return for a fee and a percentage of the profits from a privateering voyage. If a privateer was challenged, he could show the document in court to prove that his attacks were legal.

PRIVATEERS

Privateers were privately owned ships and their crews, authorized by one country to attack ships and ports of another. In the 1530s, French privateers were the first to raid the ships and poorly guarded towns of the new Spanish territories in the Caribbean. England was hostile to Spain during much of Elizabeth I's reign, so the queen encouraged her sailors to attack Spanish ships and harbors. Privateers were meant to obtain a letter of marque first and only to attack certain ships, but they often broke the rules. As some navies became stronger, privateers were not needed so often, although countries with weak navies continued to use them for hundreds of years. Many letters of marque were issued by the American states in their War of Independence against Britain. American privateers mainly operated in the West Indies and off the Newfoundland coast, but some made the long voyage to British waters. They captured at least 600 British ships. In 1856, over 50 countries agreed to end privateering, but four, including the United States, refused. Privateering was finally outlawed by all nations in 1907.

16

SIR JOHN HAWKINS

The privateer, John Hawkins, came from a family of Devon seafarers. In the 1560s, he was the first English person to make slaving voyages to the Caribbean, where he traded slaves for gold, sugar and hides. Sometimes he attacked African villages to carry off slaves, but he also robbed Portuguese ships of their slave cargoes. Although privateers were meant to attack enemy ships, England was at peace with Portugal at this time. However, there was little that could be done to stop illegal raids such as these.

Hawkins made three slaving voyages to the West Indies. Each time, the Spanish tried to stop him from unloading slaves, because they did not want other countries trading there. Hawkins took no notice and, by threatening force, landed and sold his slaves. Philip II, king of Spain, complained to Elizabeth about Hawkins, but she ignored him and even sent some of her own ships on Hawkins' voyages.

SIR FRANCIS DRAKE

Francis Drake was a relation of Hawkins. He accompanied Hawkins on an early slaving voyage, but realized that privateering was more profitable. From 1570, he attacked many Spanish ships and settlements.

In 1573, Drake attacked and robbed a mule train of 190 mules carrying Spanish treasure across the narrow Panama isthmus. He was given help by the cimarrones, former slaves from Africa, who had escaped to the mountains and lived as outlaws. Since they blamed the Spanish for enslaving them, thy were happy to help Drake. They acted as guides, carried supplies and passed on useful information.

DRAKE AND THE *CACAFUEGO*

In 1579, off the Pacific coast of Panama, Drake attacked the *Cacafuego*, a Spanish galleon packed with the largest amount of treasure ever carried on one ship. It was bound for the king of Spain, but Drake took every piece of gold, silver and precious stones. Later he seized sea charts from another Spanish ship and forced the navigators to come aboard to help him. Knowing that the Spanish expected him to return the same way he had come, Drake set sail across the immense Pacific Sea instead. With the skills and maps of the Spanish navigators to help him, he arrived in the East Indies and loaded his ship with valuable spices. Drake later threw half these spices overboard to lighten the ship when it stuck on rocks. After a journey lasting three years, Drake safely completed his circumnavigation of the world. To the dismay of the Spanish king, five tons of precious treasure were deposited for safety in the Tower of London.

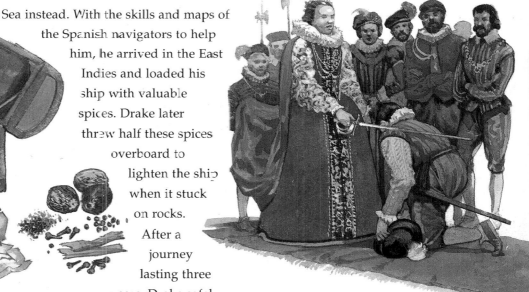

On Drake's return to England, laden with treasure and spices, the grateful queen, Elizabeth I, knighted her favorite privateer aboard his ship, the Golden Hind. Much of Drake's profit went to the queen.

17

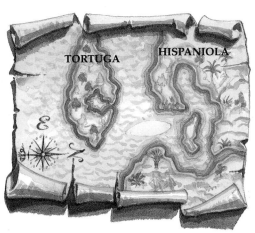

Tortuga was named after the Spanish word for a turtle, because of its shape.

BUCCANEERS

Buccaneers were originally hunters who caught wild animals on the Caribbean islands of Hispaniola and Tortuga. They skinned their prey and stretched out the hides with pegs to dry. They smoked the meat on wooden frames in huts called boucans, which gave the hunters their name as buccaneers. From the 1600s, these buccaneers were asked by island governors to carry out privateering raids on Spanish ships. As news of their successful exploits spread, others came to join them – sailors who had deserted their ships, runaway slaves and servants, and young men looking for adventure. As their numbers swelled, the buccaneers became increasingly lawless and carried out more and more raids, calling themselves the Brethren of the Coast. No one could control them as they began to target any ship, not just those belonging to enemy countries.

In the boucan strips of raw meat were laid on frames over a smoky fire, made with green sticks, bones and pieces of skin. Meat smoked like this kept for a long time and was much in demand from passing ships, in exchange for gunpowder, lead shot and alcohol.

ISLAND LIFE

The island of Tortuga was rocky and mountainous, with thick undergrowth and tall trees. Thousands of boar and cattle roamed wild, easy targets for the crackshot buccaneers with their ferocious dogs. Crabs made a tasty change from meat, but were slightly toxic and could make the men's eyesight fuzzy for a short while.

SIR HENRY MORGAN

Morgan was the Admiral of the Brethren of the Coast. In 1668, he led a surprise dawn attack on the Spanish treasure town of Portobello. His men advanced, holding the town's mayor, priests and nuns as shields in front of them. The Spanish fired anyway, killing most of the human shields. Morgan's men attacked with fireballs and the town surrendered.

FRANCOIS OLLONAIS

Ollonais was one of the most savage of all buccaneers. His real name was Jean David Nau and he had originally come to the Caribbean as a servant. In 1667, the French governor of Tortuga paid him to attack Spanish ships and towns. During his time as a buccaneer, Ollonais had many close escapes from danger. He survived a shipwreck and once hid under a pile of dead bodies to avoid being captured.

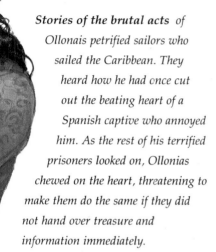

Stories of the brutal acts of Ollonais petrified sailors who sailed the Caribbean. They heard how he had once cut out the beating heart of a Spanish captive who annoyed him. As the rest of his terrified prisoners looked on, Ollonias chewed on the heart, threatening to make them do the same if they did not hand over treasure and information immediately.

19

FACT AND FICTION

⚓

Pirates in books and films often come to a violent end. This was certainly true of Ollonais, who was killed by the Darien Indians of Central America. They burned his body and scattered his ashes in the air, so that no trace of him remained.

⚓

Henry Morgan, on the other hand, ended his life in peace and comfort. King Charles II made him Deputy Governor of Jamaica in grateful thanks for his privateering services. When Morgan died in 1688, he was honored with an elaborate funeral which included a 22-gun salute.

Buccaneer clothes were hard-wearing and practical, made from animal skins, stained with blood and smelling of smoke. A large hat protected a buccaneer's head from the fierce sunshine, and bullskin leggings, with the hairy side facing inwards, protected his legs from thorny bushes. Buccaneers also carried a leather bag of food and a powder flask made from a hollowed-out gourd (a large fruit with a hard skin) covered in leather to make it waterproof.

Turtles were a much prized delicacy, especially their liver. Buccaneers rolled the turtles on to their backs, so they could pierce and kill them swiftly, using one of the long, sharp knives they always carried in their belts.

$\mathscr{S}$ HIPS

Single-masted sloops were the most popular pirate craft in the 1700s, often built in the West Indies. Between 30 and 60 feet long, they had one steeply tilted mast which could be rigged with different arrangements of sails.

SHIP TYPES

Smaller sloops and schooners could be hidden in shallow, isolated rivers for repairs, such as careening, when the hull was stripped of barnacles and weeds. Large three-masted ships had the advantage of speed and stability in bad weather. They were also more heavily armed.

Pirates never built ships to order, but sailed in whatever vessel they could seize, whether a sloop, schooner or three-masted ship. A speedy vessel was essential, so pirates could swiftly bear down on their victims and flee quickly away from anyone giving chase. A seaworthy vessel was important as it had to be strong enough to withstand foul weather and long voyages. If a seized ship did not exactly suit the pirates, they altered it to fit their purposes more precisely. Although the majority of pirates used one small sloop, the most successful pirate captains used two or more larger vessels and so were able to launch the most effective attacks. Bartholomew Roberts operated with four ships and launched 400 attacks with them, more than any other pirate. The fearsome Blackbeard operated with one ship and three large sloops. The wreck of his ship, *Queen Anne's Revenge*, was discovered recently off the eastern coast of the United States.

Two-masted schooners were slender and streamlined. The front, or bow, was sharply pointed to cut through the waves efficiently. These ships were swift and easy to maneuver because the sails were arranged in line with the hull, which made best use of the wind.

Three-masted square-rigged ships, crewed by as many as 200 pirates, were used by some of the most famous captains. These ships could be different sizes, the biggest were up to 60 feet long. Some, like the Adventure Galley, captained by Kidd, had holes for long oars, called sweeps, so that they could be rowed in calm water on windless days.

PIRATE FLAGS

The flag of an approaching pirate ship, with its gruesome images, was designed to terrify victims and encourage them to surrender. A black flag signified death and red signified battle. Some pirates designed their own flags to create even more panic.

Sometimes, pirates displayed false flags so that victims would not be aware of danger until the last moment. Pirates often stole flags from captured ships to add to their collections of false flags.

21

The skull and crossbones was only one among many popular emblems. In the 1700s, it took over as the most common pirate flag.

Roberts' flag pictured him standing astride two skulls. These represented the heads of the governors of Barbados and Martinque, Roberts' dire enemies.

FACT AND FICTION
⚓

Pirates did not always use large ships. They also attacked in small open boats, powered either by oars or a single small sail. Morgan used stolen dugout fishing canoes for his raid on Portobello. He and his men arrived at their target in them, unheard and unseen until the last moment.

⚓

The skull and crossbones flag is sometimes called the Jolly Roger. This probably comes from the French *joli rouge*, meaning *pretty red*, and dates back to a time when the usual background for the ghoulish image was red, not black.

Blackbeard's flag displayed a full length skeleton. The hourglass showed victims that time was running out. The spear pointing at a dripping heart showed victims the terrible fate that awaited them.

Jack Rackham's flag displayed a pair of crossed cutlasses and a skull. However, his flag was more terrifying than the man himself.

MONSIEUR MISSON

In 1728, Captain Charles Johnson wrote about a French pirate, Monsieur Misson, who built a fortified base on Madagascar and captured many ships. He kept two three-masted ships, but released others after stripping them of sails and rigging. Smaller craft were vandalized for ropes, timber, chains and iron.

Thomas Tew's flag featured a scimitar, a familiar weapon in the Red Sea where Tew operated.

Communication flags were used for signalling between one pirate ship and another. When pirates on one ship raised this flag, it was an invitation for pirates from nearby ships to come on board for a meeting.

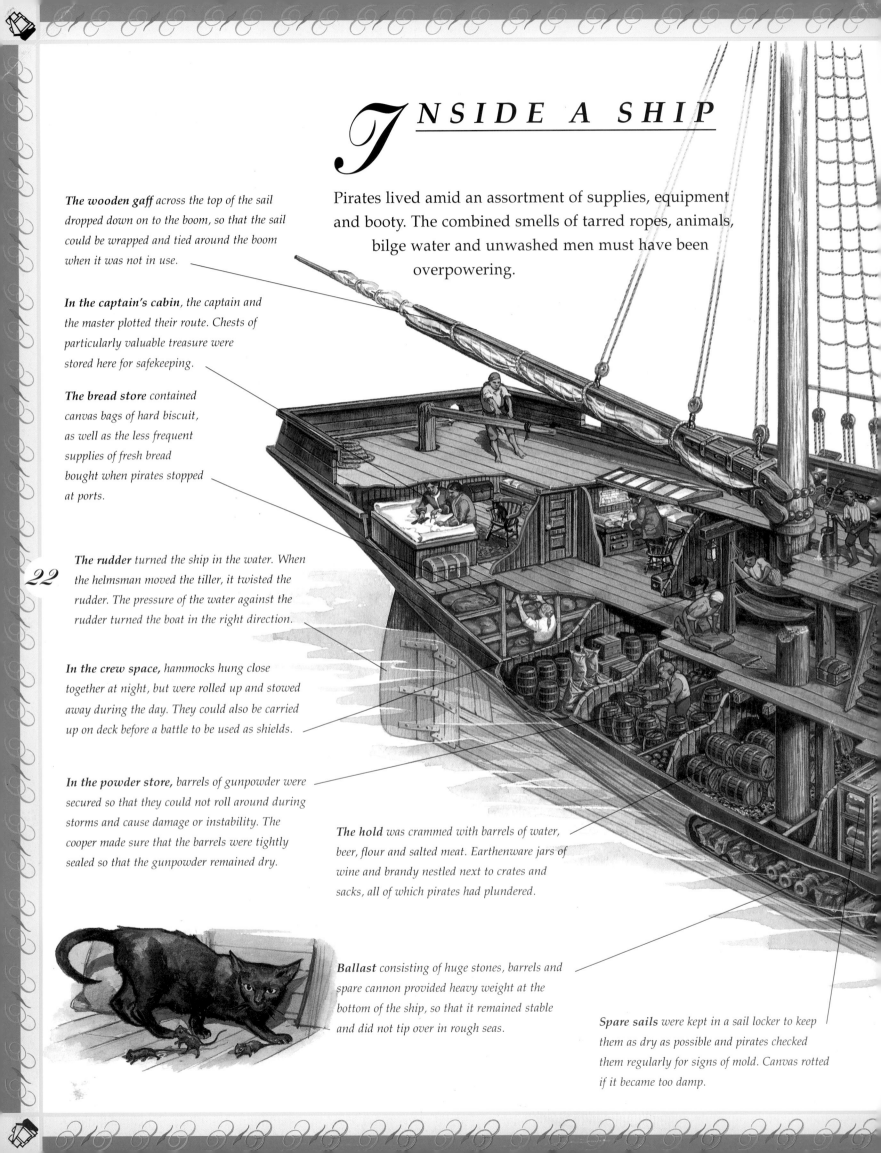

INSIDE A SHIP

Pirates lived amid an assortment of supplies, equipment and booty. The combined smells of tarred ropes, animals, bilge water and unwashed men must have been overpowering.

The wooden gaff across the top of the sail dropped down on to the boom, so that the sail could be wrapped and tied around the boom when it was not in use.

In the captain's cabin, the captain and the master plotted their route. Chests of particularly valuable treasure were stored here for safekeeping.

The bread store contained canvas bags of hard biscuit, as well as the less frequent supplies of fresh bread bought when pirates stopped at ports.

The rudder turned the ship in the water. When the helmsman moved the tiller, it twisted the rudder. The pressure of the water against the rudder turned the boat in the right direction.

In the crew space, hammocks hung close together at night, but were rolled up and stowed away during the day. They could also be carried up on deck before a battle to be used as shields.

In the powder store, barrels of gunpowder were secured so that they could not roll around during storms and cause damage or instability. The cooper made sure that the barrels were tightly sealed so that the gunpowder remained dry.

The hold was crammed with barrels of water, beer, flour and salted meat. Earthenware jars of wine and brandy nestled next to crates and sacks, all of which pirates had plundered.

Ballast consisting of huge stones, barrels and spare cannon provided heavy weight at the bottom of the ship, so that it remained stable and did not tip over in rough seas.

Spare sails were kept in a sail locker to keep them as dry as possible and pirates checked them regularly for signs of mold. Canvas rotted if it became too damp.

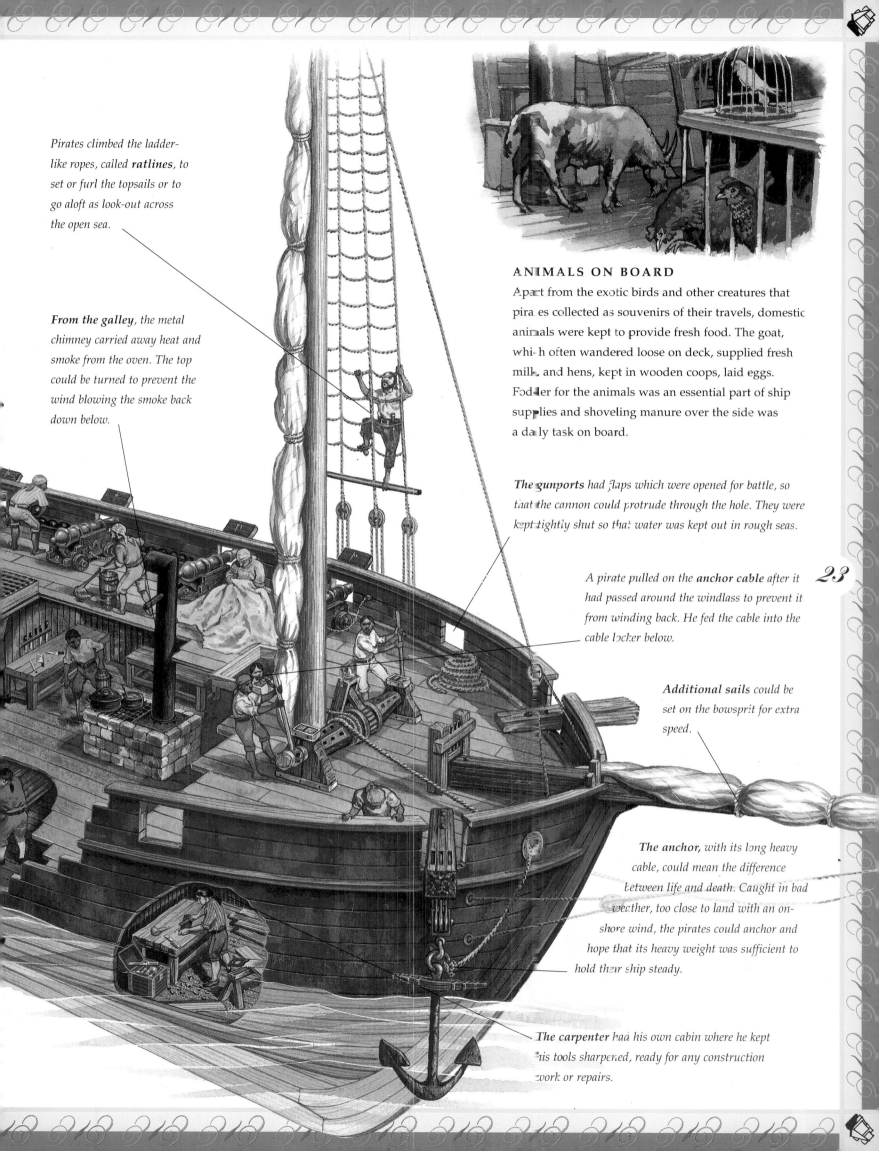

Pirates climbed the ladder-
like ropes, called **ratlines**, to
set or furl the topsails or to
go aloft as look-out across
the open sea.

From the galley, the metal
chimney carried away heat and
smoke from the oven. The top
could be turned to prevent the
wind blowing the smoke back
down below.

ANIMALS ON BOARD

Apart from the exotic birds and other creatures that
pirates collected as souvenirs of their travels, domestic
animals were kept to provide fresh food. The goat,
which often wandered loose on deck, supplied fresh
milk, and hens, kept in wooden coops, laid eggs.
Fodder for the animals was an essential part of ship
supplies and shoveling manure over the side was
a daily task on board.

The gunports had flaps which were opened for battle, so
that the cannon could protrude through the hole. They were
kept tightly shut so that water was kept out in rough seas.

A pirate pulled on the **anchor cable** after it
had passed around the windlass to prevent it
from winding back. He fed the cable into the
cable locker below.

Additional sails could be
set on the bowsprit for extra
speed.

The anchor, with its long heavy
cable, could mean the difference
between life and death. Caught in bad
weather, too close to land with an on-
shore wind, the pirates could anchor and
hope that its heavy weight was sufficient to
hold their ship steady.

The carpenter had his own cabin where he kept
his tools sharpened, ready for any construction
work or repairs.

23

The compass was consulted constantly day and night. As the iron needle turned in its ivory box, it always came to rest pointing to magnetic north, so the navigator could determine the ship's route. On long journeys, he had to remagnetize the needle by stroking it with a lodestone.

NAVIGATION

A pirate navigator needed skill and experience to cope with tides, currents and hidden rocks. He could steer a course from place to place with the aid of a compass, but only once he had pinpointed the ship's position. To do this, he needed to calculate both the ship's latitude (its position north or south of the equator), and its longitude (its position east or west of a known point). The astrolabe and the backstaff, which used the sun and stars to establish latitude, helped sailors in the 1500s but, until the late 1700s, there was no simple and accurate way to calculate longitude. Instead, the navigator used 'dead reckoning', recording in the logbook a rough estimate of the distance sailed and the compass course steered. Reliable charts were vital for long voyages and safe arrivals. If a navigator made errors in the calculations or misjudged the weather, pirates risked shipwreck.

The astrolabe was used to calculate latitude by measuring the altitude of the North Star or the noon-day sun. The center line of the astrolabe was lined up with the horizon and a sighting was taken through the two tiny holes on the pointer. It was extremely difficult to use on board ship, especially in rough seas. If the weather was cloudy, it could not be used at all, because no sightings could be taken.

The lead weight on the end of the line for measuring sea depth was filled with sticky fat. It picked up sand and shingle from the seabed, which helped pirates recognize where they were.

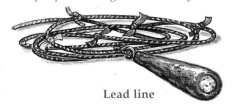

Lead line

The backstaff, like the astrolabe, was used to measure the height of the sun or North Star for calculating latitude. It had a huge advantage over the astrolabe, namely that the navigator could stand with the sun behind him, instead of looking directly into its glare.

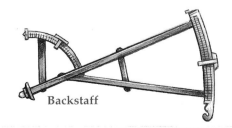

Backstaff

The log and line helped to estimate the speed of a ship. A long knotted string with a small piece of wood on one end was wound around a reel. The piece of wood was thrown over the back of the ship, so that the line unwound as the ship traveled forward. By counting the knots on the line as a sand glass emptied, the navigator could work out the ship's approximate speed. A larger glass recorded how long a ship had been traveling.

Sand glass

Lines of latitude and longitude are imaginary lines marked on sea charts in a grid. Horizontal latitude lines run parallel with the equator, and the lines of longitude run at right angles to them. Sailors use these as coordinates to pinpoint the precise position of their ship. Before an accurate method of establishing longitude was found, 'running along a line of latitude' was an accepted way of navigating.

A nautical ruler and dividers were used to record the ship's route every day on to a chart. Using a compass to establish a ship's course, a hour glass to measure time, and a log and line to estimate speed, the navigator calculated the movement of the ship and plotted it on the chart. This was crucial in cloudy weather, when neither the sun nor stars could be seen.

The octant was not invented until 1731. Although far more accurate than earlier instruments, it was also much more complicated, so only the most skilled navigators mastered its use. Because the octant measured both horizontal and vertical angles, it could be used to take both bearings of landmarks and sightings of heavenly bodies.

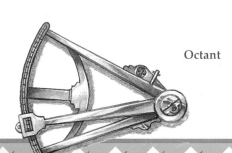

Octant

BARTHOLOMEW SHARP

Bartholomew Sharp led a group of pirates who plundered Spanish settlements along the Pacific coast of South America. In 1681, during an attack on a Spanish ship, the *Rosario*, the crew tried to throw their charts overboard, but Sharp snatched them back. The Spanish were so distressed by this disaster that they wept. England and Spain were at peace at this time, so Sharp should have faced punishment for his piratical activities. However, at a time when England possessed no accurate maps of the Pacific Ocean, the king, Charles II, recognized their value and pardoned him.

WORK ON BOARD

Routine work on board a sailing ship was hard and sometimes dangerous, especially in rough weather. Pirates needed to be physically tough and many of them were relatively young, usually under the age of thirty. Many had grown up in ports of different countries and had been sailors from an early age. Much of their work was boring and repetitive, such as taking in and letting out the sails, working the bilge pumps, swabbing the decks or keeping watch. Sails and ropes needed constant repairs. However, since pirate crews were often much larger than the crew of a merchant ship of the same size, there were many more men to share the work. Carpenters and coopers did more skilled work, so on some ships they received a larger share of the profits.

The captain *was in command during battle, but between attacks important decisions were taken by the whole crew. A captain faced being ousted if he misused his authority. When pirate captain, Charles Vane, refused to attack a well-defended French ship, his crew voted for their quartermaster, Jack Rackham, to take his place. The quartermaster was an important figure who represented the views of the crew, and enforced discipline.*

yard

ratlines

Unfurling the sails *needed a head for heights and a good sense of balance. On a square-rigged ship, sailors climbed the ratlines to reach the yards on which the sails were set. Once aloft, they had only a thin rope suspended from the yard to stand upon.*

Measuring the sea depth *was one of the sailing master's tasks. Tied to the rigging to prevent him falling overboard, he swung a long rope weighted with lead into the water. When the lead hit the seabed, he could tell, by looking at the different fabric markers tied at equal lengths along the rope, how deep the water was.*

The windlass *gave additional power for heavy jobs, such as lifting the anchor and hoisting heavy cargo aboard. A sailor at each end of the windlass levered a long-handled crank, which turned the cylinder and wound a rope cable.*

Mending sails *was skilled work. It was vital that sails were repaired carefully, so that tears did not spread and flap in strong winds. The sailmaker wore a protective leather palm with a metal disc in the center. This helped him force the needle through the heavy canvas sailcloth.*

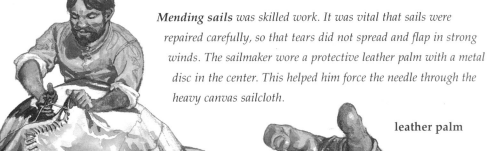

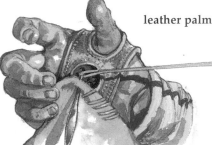

leather palm

Swabbing the decks was a daily task. Otherwise they could become very slippery, which could cause accidents and even prove fatal during fights.

A look-out was always on duty high above the deck clinging to the ratlines. He scanned the sea with a telescope for any sign of enemies or possible victims.

The cooper was skilled at making, repairing and sealing the barrels in which much of the ship's food and drink was stored. His was an important job, since food stored in poorly constructed or badly sealed barrels rotted quickly.

The helmsman steered the ship with the tiller, following the direction chosen by the navigator. As he moved the tiller from side to side, it turned the rudder.

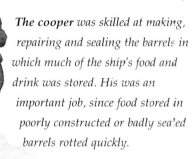

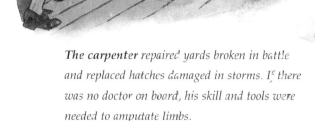

pitch ladle

hot pitch

The carpenter repaired yards broken in battle and replaced hatches damaged in storms. If there was no doctor on board, his skill and tools were needed to amputate limbs.

The caulker kept the ship as watertight as possible. He opened up any gaps between rotten planks with a ramming iron, hammered in a filling of oakum (rope fibers) and sealed this with hot pitch.

Bilge pumps cleared the water that had seeped through the planking and collected in the bottom of the ship. As a sailor worked the pump handle up and down, the foul, stinking water was pumped on to the deck. It ran over the side through the scuppers (drain holes).

gouge

auger

ramming iron

caulking mallet

CLOTHES

THE CAPTAIN'S CLOTHES

A pirate captain kept a choice of several outfits stored in a sea chest in his cabin. Pirates did not usually wear their best clothes for fighting, but kept them pristine for showing off ashore.

Wigs were worn by gentlemen from 1660 onwards. Since these were expensive and hot to wear, pirate captains grew their hair long instead, and wore it tied back with a ribbon.

Gold buttons carved with intricate patterns added extra decoration to the captain's outfit. It was fashionable to leave most of the coat buttons undone so that the waistcoat could be admired.

Silver buckles were used both to decorate leather shoes and to fasten the legs of breeches. Some buckles were so elaborate they looked like jewelry.

Rolls of stolen fabric were prized. Glossy taffeta could be made into fine breeches and velvet was used for coats.

Fine French lace was sewn on to cuffs and collars as trimming.

Pirate leaders, like other ship captains, liked to dress differently from their crew and often wore fashionable clothes made of expensive fabrics, such as silk, lace and velvet. Some wore clothes that made them look like smart gentlemen or officers in the navy. Others preferred a fancier look and wore exotic outfits put together from garments stolen from different victims. The crew, on the other hand, needed to wear clothes that were both hardwearing and comfortable for working, climbing ships' rigging and fighting. Most pirates wore clothes similar to those of ordinary sailors. However, since there was no naval uniform at the time, sailors did not all dress alike. Many pirates acquired clothes during attacks. Captured sailors were forced to strip off particular garments that took a pirate's fancy. Women were not normally allowed on board pirate ships. Those who managed to become pirates succeeded by disguising themselves in men's clothes.

BARTHOLOMEW ROBERTS

This pirate captain, active in the 1720s, dressed in clothes that were the height of fashion. His matching coat, waistcoat and breeches were made of crimson damask, a special silk with a woven pattern. Wearing red was a particular sign of wealth, since the dye was made from expensive crushed cochineal beetles from Mexico. Roberts added a red feather to his hat and wore a gold chain with a glittering diamond cross around his neck. He hung his pistols from a silk sling worn over his shoulders. For his final battle off the hot and humid west coast of Africa, Roberts dressed in his most splendid outfit.

ANNE BONNY

Anne Bonny had dressed in boy's clothes since she was a child, when her father disguised her so that he could train her as a lawyer's clerk. When she grew up, she married a sailor and traveled to the West Indies. There she met Calico Jack and joined his pirate crew. Since pirate ships had severe punishments if women were found on board, Anne disguised herself in men's clothes, grew her hair in the same style and used the same weapons as the other pirates.

CALICO JACK RACKHAM

Jack Rackham was nicknamed Calico Jack, because he dressed in brightly colored clothes made from stolen calico. His ship was only a small sloop, so he sensibly limited his choice of victims to fishing boats and small craft carrying local goods. His crew of twelve pirates, including Anne Bonny and Mary Read, another woman pirate, all wore similar clothes – dark jackets, long trousers and handkerchiefs around their necks. He was reputed to treat his victims kindly, and the two female pirates accused him of not fighting fiercely enough during their final battle.

THE CLOTHES OF AN ORDINARY PIRATE

The pirate crew usually had only one outfit of clothes each. The only items they washed regularly were their cotton shirts, which dried quickly. The rest were usually stained, often torn and almost certainly very smelly. When a garment became really disgusting, a pirate bought or stole another one to replace it.

A scarf or kerchief tied around a pirate's head helped to keep out dirt and dust. It could also be rolled and tied around the forehead as a bandana during a battle, to keep sweat from running down the face.

A cravat of muslin or silk kept a pirate's neck warm and absorbed sweat.

Buttons were made of bone and wood.

The long, warm loose-fitting jacket was always made in a dark color, usually blue.

FACT AND FICTION
⚓

Pirates in films often wear clothes that were fashionable at the time of the Restoration of the English king, Charles II, in 1660. Caribbean pirates were particularly active throughout his reign.

⚓

In his play, *Peter Pan*, James Barrie made his villainous pirate, Captain Hook, resemble Charles II, including his long black curly wig. A real pirate would never have fought in such a cumbersome wig.

A wide sash was worn around the waist. Red silk was a popular choice.

Trousers were wide and comfortable for easy movement. They were made of a type of cotton called calico.

The long, warm loose-fitting jacket was always made in a dark color, usually blue.

Shoes were made of leather and had high tongues and large buckles. Some pirates worked and fought on board ship in bare feet, which gave better grip when the deck was slippery.

29

LIFE ON BOARD

DOWN BELOW

Pirates ate their meals in the Great Cabin, which the captain was expected to share with the rest of his crew. Mealtimes were often very rowdy, as pirates drank heavily, sharing punch from a huge silver bowl or drinking wine from pewter tankards.

In many ways, a pirate's life on board resembled that of any sailor. Living spaces were airless, cramped and often overcrowded, and there was no privacy for washing or shaving. In the Caribbean, fresh turtle, fish and pigs provided nutritious meals but, on long voyages, there was a lack of fresh food or water. However, with no deadlines to meet or cargoes to be delivered, and more hands than usual to do daily tasks, pirates had far more time to enjoy eating, drinking and amusements. Captured seamen were often attracted by the more relaxed life on board a pirate ship and willingly joined their crew. Heavy drinking could lead to violent behavior, but the closeness of life on board also led to life-long friendships.

On long voyages, pirates mainly ate dried or salted meat and dry ships' biscuits. These biscuits were often infested with writhing maggots and crawling weevils.

PERSONAL LIFE

Pirates slept in hammocks below deck. On hot nights, they slept on the open deck. Bedtime was surprisingly early – all lights and candles were supposed to be put out at 8 o'clock. Those who wanted to make merry until late went on deck under the watchful eye of the quartermaster. Personal belongings, such as shaving equipment and snuff boxes, were kept in sea chests. Pirates sniffed snuff rather than smoking a pipe because it was safer on board wooden ships which carried explosives.

GAMES

Cards and dice could lead to violent quarrels as bets were often involved. In 1703, the pirates of Captain Woodes Rogers' ship signed an agreement banning all gambling.

MUSIC AND DANCING

Energetic dancing and singing to the music of the fiddle helped to pass the long periods of time between raids. Bartholomew Roberts made sure that his musicians had a day off on the Sabbath Day (Sunday), by including a rule about it in his pirate code (see page 33).

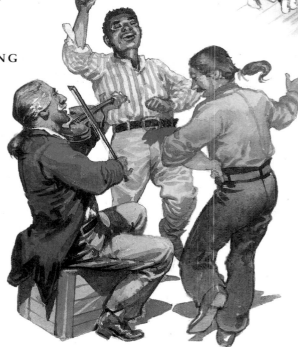

COOKING

The ship's cook prepared meals in the galley on a brick stove with a metal chimney. The large store of wood needed to fuel the stove added to the general clutter on board. The crew collected firewood whenever they landed at suitably wooded spots. The cook always kept a container of sand nearby, in case of fire which could spread rapidly on a wooden ship.

$\mathscr{D}$ISCIPLINE

Rules and punishments to maintain good discipline on board were as necessary on a pirate ship as any other. However, pirates organized themselves in a very different way from merchant and naval crews. They voted democratically on all aspects of their activities, elected their own captain and quartermaster and could remove them if they were unhappy with their leadership. The rules were agreed by everyone and put down in writing. These set out how prizes were to be divided and the amounts of compensation for injuries. They also listed punishments for breaking rules. Offenses against fellow pirates were regarded as particularly serious, punishable by marooning. Other punishments, such as keel-hauling and flogging, although brutal, were used less frequently than on ordinary ships. If discovered, written rules provided hard evidence of piracy that could be used against pirates in court, so they were usually destroyed before they could be captured. Exceptionally, Captain Bartholomew Roberts' rules survive.

Water

Musket

Shot

Powder flask

THE CASTAWAY

The punishment for any pirate who robbed another pirate or who abandoned his post in battle was marooning. Put ashore on an isolated island or stretch of coastline, the lonely castaway had to fend for himself or starve. If he had robbed another pirate, his ears and nose might also have been slit. The only equipment allowed was a bottle of fresh water, and a musket with a flask of gunpowder and a few lead shots. These would only last a few days. Thereafter, the mariner had to forage for food. He tried to spear fish on sticks, but relied mainly on roots, nuts and berries. Alexander Selkirk was a real castaway sailor who was fictionalized, in 1719, by Daniel Defoe in *Robinson Crusoe*. Selkirk asked to be put ashore, because he was tired of life at sea. He lived alone on a deserted island near Chile for more than four years.

PUNISHMENTS ON BOARD

Harsh punishments were listed in some pirate rules but, in practice, were rarely enforced. However, after capturing a ship, pirates often asked its crew about the discipline on board. If they reported unfair or extreme treatment, the pirates were quite likely to give the captain a taste of his own medicine.

Flogging was carried out in view of the entire company. Captains who had treated their own sailors badly were stripped to the waist, tied to a grating and lashed with a cat o' nine tails.

During keel-hauling, the unfortunate sailor was bound hand and foot to a rope. As he was hauled under the ship from one side to the other, his flesh was scraped raw by the sharp barnacles on the sides of the ship. This punishment dated back to the Greeks.

The cat o' nine tails was a wooden stick covered with cloth. It had nine knotted tails of twisted rope, which cut searingly into the skin.

FACT AND FICTION
⚓
Cunning Blackbeard used marooning as an excuse to rid himself of unwanted crew members. That way, he would receive a larger share of any profits himself.
⚓
There is no evidence that pirates made their victims walk the plank. Although this is a popular fictional punishment, in real life it was much quicker simply to hurl unfortunate prisoners overboard.

33

ROBERTS' RULES

1 Each pirate shall have an equal vote, and all will receive an equal share of food and drink seized.

2 Each pirate in turn will have first choice of plunder, but those who cheat their fellow pirates will be marooned.

3 No pirate will wager money on cards or dice games aboard ship.

4 Candles and lanterns will be extinguished at eight o'clock. Pirates awake after this hour shall sit up on unlit deck.

5 Each pirate vows to keep cutlass and all other arms clean and ready for use at all times.

6 No women pirates are allowed. The penalty for bringing a disguised woman on board is death.

7 Desertion during battle shall be punished by death or marooning.

8 Pirates will not fight each other on board. Quarrels will be settled ashore by duel, overseen by the quartermaster.

9 Every pirate who loses a limb will be paid compensation.

10 The captain and the quartermaster will receive a double share of all prizes.

11 The musicians shall not work on the Sabbath Day.

ILLNESS & INJURY

Pirates risked injury in every battle. Even minor wounds could become infected with fatal results. Severe injuries could end a pirate's career, so crews set aside money to compensate those who lost fingers, eyes or limbs in battle or during accidents at work. Illness could be just as dangerous as injury at a time when hygiene and medical treatments were poor. On long journeys, a lack of vitamin C caused terrible scurvy. Sufferers' bleeding gums sometimes swelled so much that they covered the teeth. Malaria, dysentery and fever were also common. Mary Read, for example, escaped execution, but died of fever in prison. A skilled surgeon who could treat illness and injury was highly valued. Without one, operations were sometimes carried out by the ship's carpenter. Surgeons on captured ships were sometimes forced to enlist with pirates, bring their prized medicine chests and tools with them.

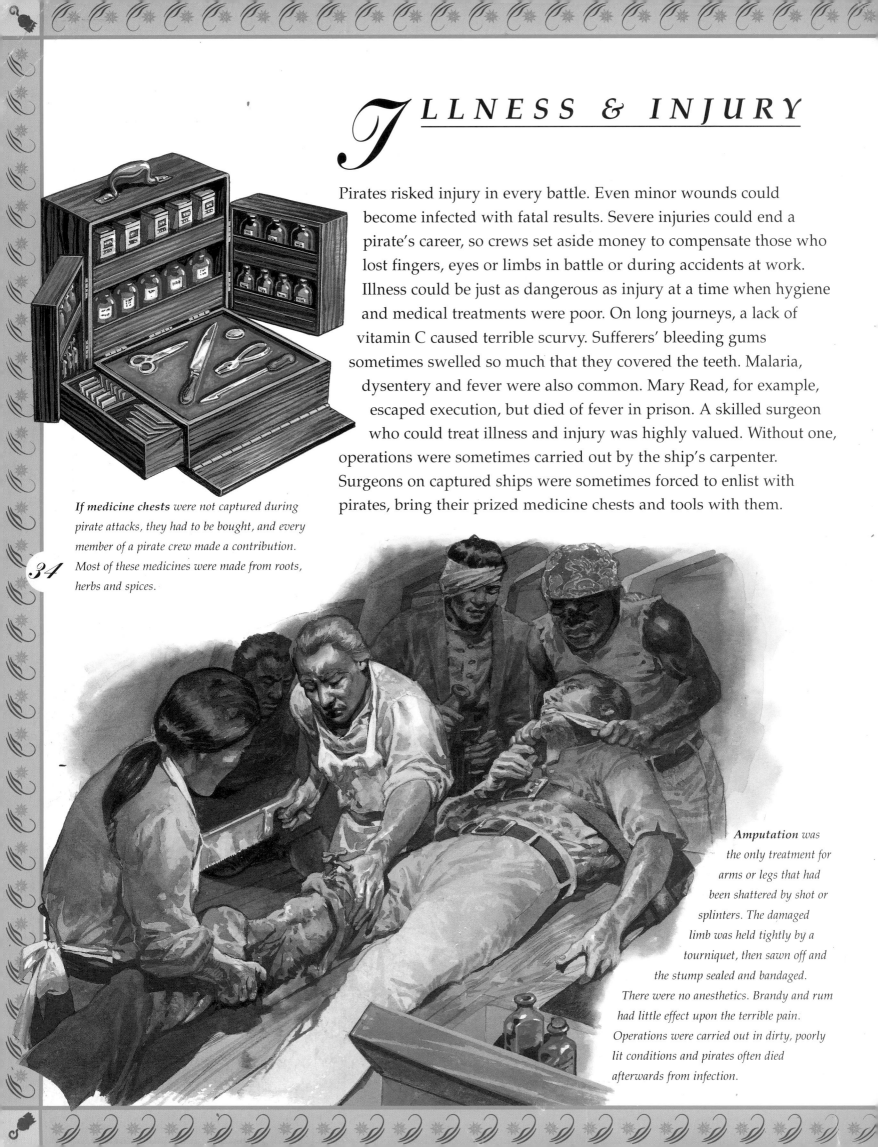

If medicine chests were not captured during pirate attacks, they had to be bought, and every member of a pirate crew made a contribution. Most of these medicines were made from roots, herbs and spices.

34

Amputation was the only treatment for arms or legs that had been shattered by shot or splinters. The damaged limb was held tightly by a tourniquet, then sawn off and the stump sealed and bandaged. There were no anesthetics. Brandy and rum had little effect upon the terrible pain. Operations were carried out in dirty, poorly lit conditions and pirates often died afterwards from infection.

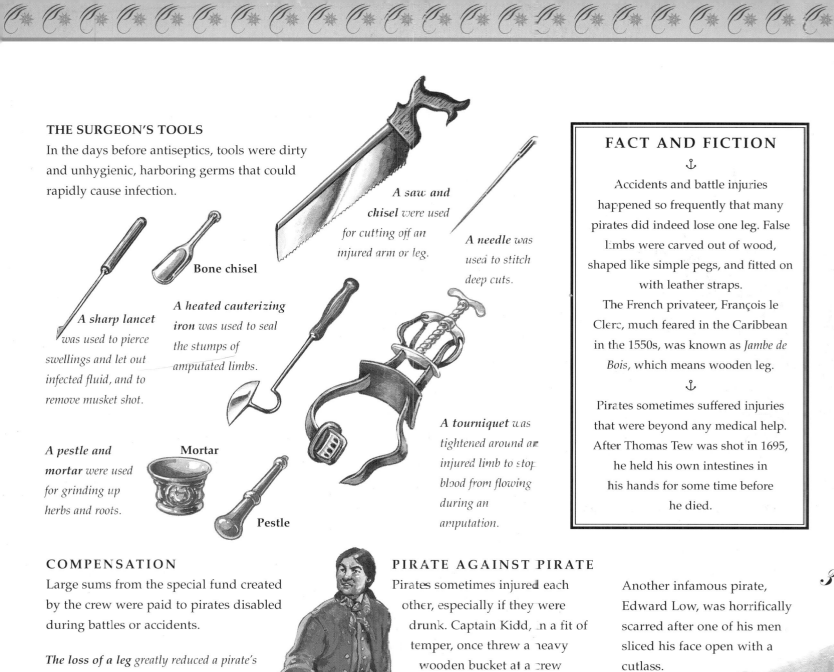

THE SURGEON'S TOOLS

In the days before antiseptics, tools were dirty and unhygienic, harboring germs that could rapidly cause infection.

A saw and chisel were used for cutting off an injured arm or leg.

Bone chisel

A needle was used to stitch deep cuts.

A sharp lancet was used to pierce swellings and let out infected fluid, and to remove musket shot.

A heated cauterizing iron was used to seal the stumps of amputated limbs.

Mortar

A pestle and mortar were used for grinding up herbs and roots.

Pestle

A tourniquet was tightened around an injured limb to stop blood from flowing during an amputation.

FACT AND FICTION

⚓

Accidents and battle injuries happened so frequently that many pirates did indeed lose one leg. False limbs were carved out of wood, shaped like simple pegs, and fitted on with leather straps.

The French privateer, François le Clerc, much feared in the Caribbean in the 1550s, was known as *Jambe de Bois*, which means wooden leg.

⚓

Pirates sometimes suffered injuries that were beyond any medical help. After Thomas Tew was shot in 1695, he held his own intestines in his hands for some time before he died.

COMPENSATION

Large sums from the special fund created by the crew were paid to pirates disabled during battles or accidents.

The loss of a leg greatly reduced a pirate's ability to make a living on either land or sea. A pirate who lost his right leg was paid 500 pieces of eight, while a lost left leg was priced at 400 pieces of eight. Pirates disabled like this sometimes became a pirate ship's cook.

The loss of an arm caused a pirate even greater incapacity, so higher payments were made. Compensation of 600 pieces of eight was paid for a right arm and 500 for a left arm. The 16th-century corsair, Aruj Barbarossa, lost an arm after he was wounded in battle against the Spanish. As a result of being disabled, he lost his dominance and his younger brother became far more powerful.

PIRATE AGAINST PIRATE

Pirates sometimes injured each other, especially if they were drunk. Captain Kidd, in a fit of temper, once threw a heavy wooden bucket at a crew member. It broke the man's skull and killed him.

Another infamous pirate, Edward Low, was horrifically scarred after one of his men sliced his face open with a cutlass.

35

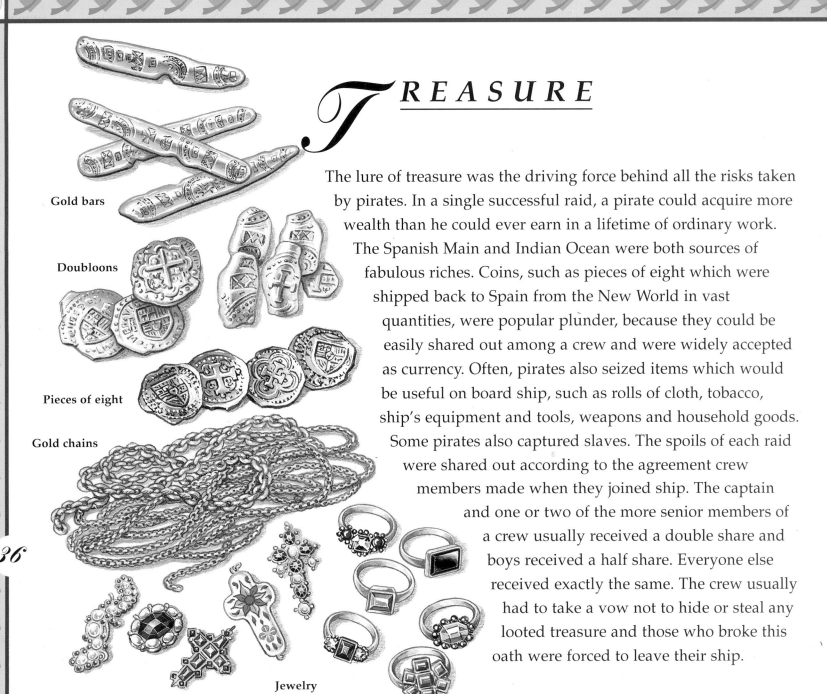

TREASURE

Gold bars

Doubloons

Pieces of eight

Gold chains

Jewelry

The lure of treasure was the driving force behind all the risks taken by pirates. In a single successful raid, a pirate could acquire more wealth than he could ever earn in a lifetime of ordinary work. The Spanish Main and Indian Ocean were both sources of fabulous riches. Coins, such as pieces of eight which were shipped back to Spain from the New World in vast quantities, were popular plunder, because they could be easily shared out among a crew and were widely accepted as currency. Often, pirates also seized items which would be useful on board ship, such as rolls of cloth, tobacco, ship's equipment and tools, weapons and household goods. Some pirates also captured slaves. The spoils of each raid were shared out according to the agreement crew members made when they joined ship. The captain and one or two of the more senior members of a crew usually received a double share and boys received a half share. Everyone else received exactly the same. The crew usually had to take a vow not to hide or steal any looted treasure and those who broke this oath were forced to leave their ship.

Gold and silver produced in the Americas were a rich prize for pirates. Gold bars were stamped with marks which showed where each one was made, its quality, and the amount of tax paid on it. Gold coins minted in the Americas were much rarer than silver pieces of eight. Rich passengers often possessed doubloons from Spain, worth more than any other gold coins, as well as fine jewelry. Their gold chains could be separated into individual links and used as money. Jewelry was a particularly popular loot, because it was small, light and easy to carry.

Ships' stores were looted for wooden casks of wine and beer as well as earthenware bottles of brandy. Tobacco twists were snatched from victim crews for smoking, chewing or making snuff.

Tobacco twists

Alcohol

Brandy

36

Practical household goods, such as cooking pots, candles and spare sails, were often carried away during a raid. Each pirate was also entitled to take a set of clothing from crew members of a captured ship, and they took it in turns to have first pick. Rolls of silk and lace were stolen either to sell or for making into clothes.

CAPTAIN KIDD

Captain William Kidd was unusual for a pirate because he came from a wealthy English family and had many influential friends. Like many other pirates, he had previously been a privateer. In 1698, he captured a large merchant ship, the *Quedah Merchant*, in the Indian Ocean. Its valuable cargo included silk, sugar and opium, which Kidd sold to eager merchants for thousands of pounds.

SPENDING THE PROFITS

Few pirates ever retired to live quietly on the proceeds of their crimes. Much of the loot they acquired so quickly was spent equally quickly on wine and women in the Caribbean pirate ports of Jamaica and New Providence. Pirates who returned to remote pirate bases, such as Madagascar, after successful raids found it impossible to sell all their fabulous loot. Several of them, including Kidd and Tew, preferred to risk capture by going to America and the Caribbean to convert their booty into cash.

FACT AND FICTION

⚓

Buried treasure features prominently in many fictional pirate stories, but there are very few real examples. Captain Kidd inspired the belief by burying several bags of coins and wooden chests from the *Quedah Merchant* on a small island near New York. Most of it was recovered, but nonetheless stories continued to circulate that there was more of Kidd's fabulous treasure still to be found.

$\mathcal{W}$EAPONS

BATTLES ON DECK
Hand-to-hand fighting was loud, vicious and undisciplined, and the pirates' weapons inflicted terrible wounds.

Pirates were renowned for being heavily armed, whereas their victims usually had few weapons. Often the thought of well-armed pirates was enough for a ship's captain to surrender very swiftly, sometimes without any fight at all. Before they launched an attack, pirates often fired a warning shot from one of their cannon, rather than firing them all at once. They aimed at the masts or rigging, so that they did not sink a ship that might make a good prize. As they came closer to their prey, pirates hurled iron balls with hooks into the rigging to damage it further. If a ship still refused to surrender, grenades were thrown on board. These caused injury and confusion. When the ship was in range of musket fire, pirates with the truest aim shot at individual sailors. Once the pirates were finally close enough to clamber on board their unlucky victims' ship, they wielded their flintlock pistols, daggers and cutlasses against anyone who resisted them.

38

A flintlock musket was used to shoot targets at a distance. Several of them, well-aimed and fired together, could be as effective as a cannon.

Musket balls were made of lead. They were loaded singly, wrapped in a small patch of cloth.

A grenade was a hollow glass or iron container, filled with gunpowder. When it exploded, lethal fragments flew everywhere.

Earthenware stinkpots filled with lit sulphur were thrown on deck. The smoke choked the sailors and made their eyes stream with tears.

Gunpowder was kept in horns or small leather flasks with metal lids. If it became damp, it was useless.

Grappling hooks were tied to the end of long ropes securely fixed on the piates' ship. Pirates threw them on to the rigging of their victims' ship, so they could haul their own ship closer.

A boarding axe was useful for helping pirates haul themselves up the steep sides of their victims' ships. Once aboard, pirates then used the axes to slash the sails and rigging, so that the ship would be unable to sail away.

39

FACT AND FICTION
⚓

Real pirates did indeed carry as many weapons as they could manage – at least two pistols, a cutlass and dagger. A pistol could be fired only once before re-loading, so it made good sense to carry several.

⚓

Blackbeard's sailing master was called Israel Hands. Once, during a game of cards, Blackbeard suddenly blew out all the candles and opened fire in the dark. Israel Hands was shot in the knees and limped for the rest of his life. Robert Louis Stevenson borrowed his name for one of the fictional pirates in his book, *Treasure Island*.

A baldrick was worn around a pirate's waist or across his chest. Spare powder charges were tucked into this special leather belt.

A sword was too long for fighting on board a crowded ship, but was often used in land attacks instead.

flint

barrel

flash pan | trigger

A flintlock pistol was used for firing at close quarters. It was light to carry, but slow to load. Powder and a lead ball were rammed down the barrel. More powder was poured into the flash pan. When the trigger was pulled, a spark from the flint lit the powder. This exploded and fired the lead ball.

BLACKBEARD

Edward Teach, better known as Blackbeard, was one of the most frightening pirates a sailor could have the misfortune to meet. He carried six pistols, as well as a sword and cutlass. He was a huge man with fierce, wild and bloodshot eyes. He had a mass of tangled hair, which to one observer looked like 'a frightful meteor' and a beard which came up to his eyes and reached down to his waist. He twisted both his hair and beard into tails and bound them in black ribbons. In battle, he made himself look even more fearsome by plaiting hemp fuse cords into his hair and under his hat. When he lit these cords they slowly smoldered, surrounding his head with smoke. During raids, he carried his cutlass between his teeth as he scaled the side of a ship.

cutlass

A cutlass with a sharp broad blade and a **thin dagger** were the most practical weapons for close fighting on board ship, because they were short.

dagger

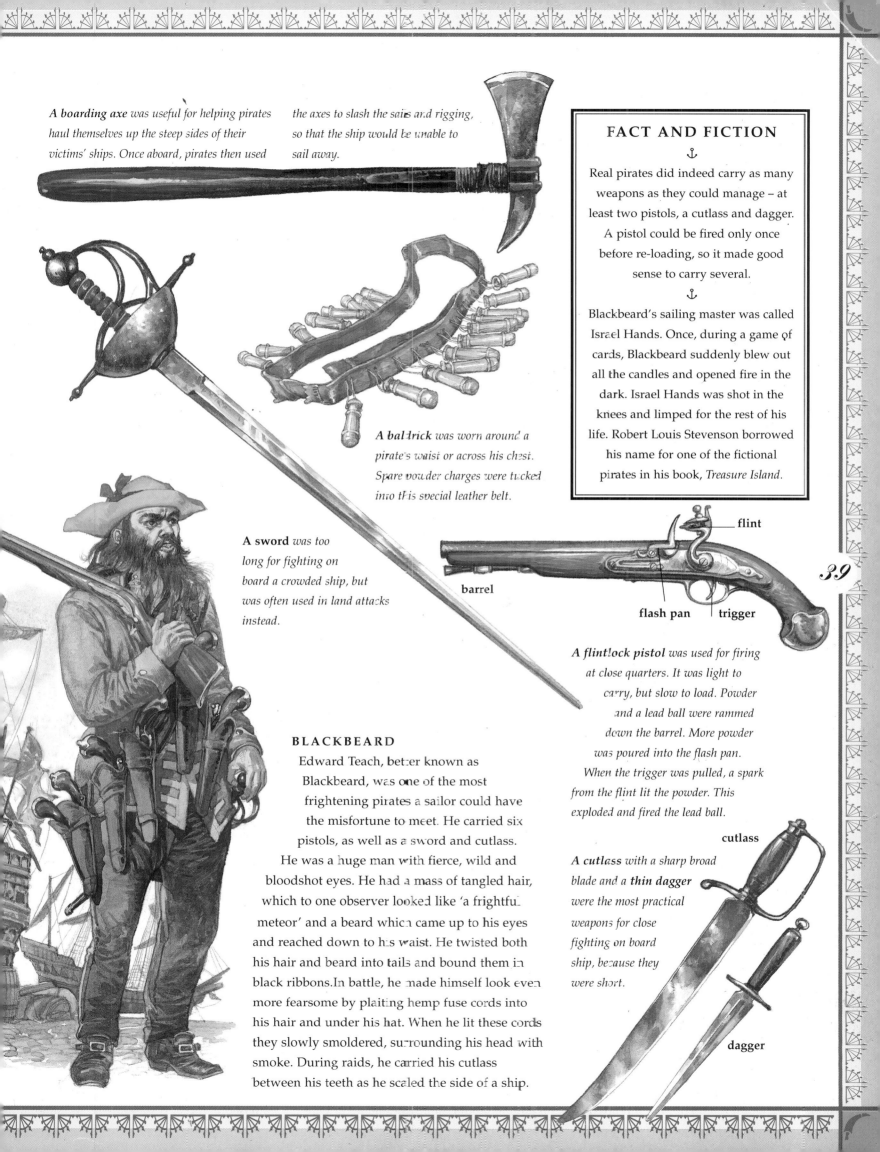

ATTACK

Pirates did not attack every ship they encountered. When they spotted a potential target, they considered carefully whether or not they could defeat it easily. If most of the crew agreed to attack, then they went swiftly into action. Speed and surprise were vital if their ship was to sail within range without causing alarm. The victims were powerless to escape once the masts and sails of their ship had been damaged by heavy shot from the pirates' cannon. As a desperate last minute delaying tactic, some captains spread broken glass on deck, even if boarding by pirates was unavoidable. Coming under attack by pirates was horrific, whether or not fighting was avoided. The looters ransacked their victims' ship from top to bottom, threatening passengers with brutality or torture if they did not reveal the whereabouts of their valuables.

Before they boarded, *pirates aimed to intimidate the crew as much as possible. They tossed small pots filled with burning oil on to the deck. The loud commotion of their shouts and cries, coupled with their terrifying reputation meant that attacks often succeeded without large-scale fighting.*

Violence was usually avoided if sailors surrendered immediately. However, if they resisted, many pirates were prepared to be brutal to get their way. As a final resort, uncooperative crew members were thrown over the side of the ship.

Forcing surgeons, coopers and carpenters to join a raiding pirate crew was common. If they refused to bring their tools and leave voluntarily, ways were found to persuade them. One unlucky cooper was beaten with an axe handle and threatened with beheading before he agreed to enlist.

Looting could be carried out at a leisurely pace because victims had no way to summon help quickly. Pirates searched the ship's hold for saleable cargoes, emptied the lockers and examined the sailors' sleeping quarters for useful possessions. Wealthy travelers, frightened for their lives, led pirates to their cabins and showed them where their jewels and other valuables were hidden.

THE CANNON

Although pirate ships carried more cannon than the merchant ships they targeted, they were no match for the full firepower of a naval ship. Cannon balls, bar and chain struck the sides of ships with immense impact, causing horrific injuries to those on board.

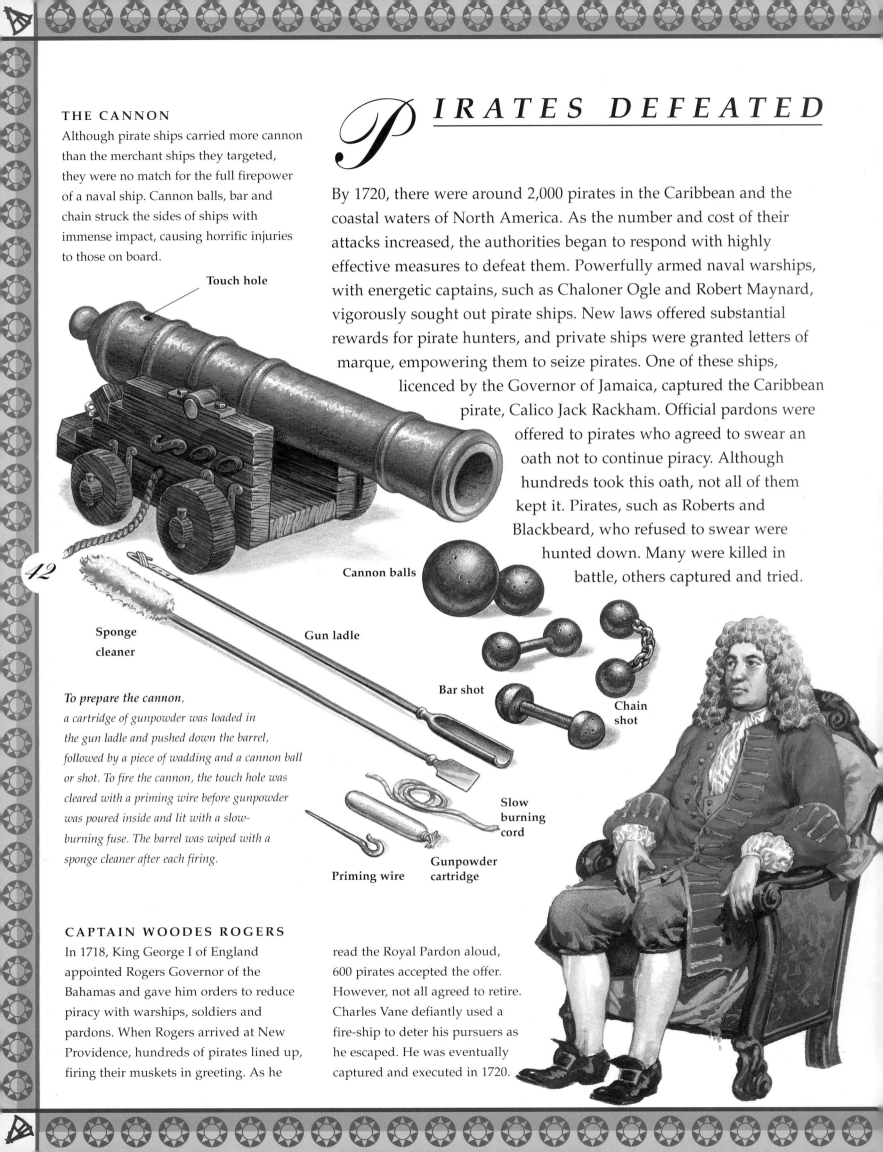

Touch hole

42

Cannon balls

Sponge cleaner

Gun ladle

To prepare the cannon,
a cartridge of gunpowder was loaded in
the gun ladle and pushed down the barrel,
followed by a piece of wadding and a cannon ball
or shot. To fire the cannon, the touch hole was
cleared with a priming wire before gunpowder
was poured inside and lit with a slow-
burning fuse. The barrel was wiped with a
sponge cleaner after each firing.

Bar shot

Chain shot

Slow burning cord

Priming wire

Gunpowder cartridge

PIRATES DEFEATED

By 1720, there were around 2,000 pirates in the Caribbean and the coastal waters of North America. As the number and cost of their attacks increased, the authorities began to respond with highly effective measures to defeat them. Powerfully armed naval warships, with energetic captains, such as Chaloner Ogle and Robert Maynard, vigorously sought out pirate ships. New laws offered substantial rewards for pirate hunters, and private ships were granted letters of marque, empowering them to seize pirates. One of these ships, licenced by the Governor of Jamaica, captured the Caribbean pirate, Calico Jack Rackham. Official pardons were offered to pirates who agreed to swear an oath not to continue piracy. Although hundreds took this oath, not all of them kept it. Pirates, such as Roberts and Blackbeard, who refused to swear were hunted down. Many were killed in battle, others captured and tried.

CAPTAIN WOODES ROGERS

In 1718, King George I of England appointed Rogers Governor of the Bahamas and gave him orders to reduce piracy with warships, soldiers and pardons. When Rogers arrived at New Providence, hundreds of pirates lined up, firing their muskets in greeting. As he read the Royal Pardon aloud, 600 pirates accepted the offer. However, not all agreed to retire. Charles Vane defiantly used a fire-ship to deter his pursuers as he escaped. He was eventually captured and executed in 1720.

CAPTAIN CHALONER OGLE

In 1722, Ogle set sail in HMS *Swallow* on the trail of Bartholomew Roberts. When Ogle spotted the pirate's three ships off the western coast of Africa, he set a trap. He sailed away as if he were the captain of a merchant ship frightened of attack. Roberts sent one of his ships to give chase. By the time the pirates realized they had been tricked it was too late – their ship was already within range of the warship's heavy cannon.

THE FALL OF ROBERTS

Ogle repeated this trick equally successfully with the pirate commander. Again, Roberts failed to recognise Ogle's ship until the last moment, but decided to face his pursuer rather than flee. In driving rain, his crew of 150 on the *Royal Fortune* fought hard, but could not defeat Ogle's superior armed power. Early in the battle, Roberts was shot in the neck and killed. His crew continued to resist bombardment without their leader but, after hours of fighting, they all finally surrendered. Ogle was knighted by King George I for his part in Roberts' downfall.

Roberts' body was thrown overboard by his crew, as he had requested if he died. He hated the thought that the authorities might display his body as a deterrent to others.

THE DEATH OF BLACKBEARD

Blackbeard was defiant to the end. When some of his crew became ill, he seized hostages from Charleston, South Carolina and held them until the town handed over a medicine chest. Later, two naval sloops pursued him and a fierce battle ensued. Blackbeard boarded one of the sloops, believing its crew had been slaughtered, but they surged up from their hiding places below and took Blackbeard by surprise. Lieutenant Maynard cut the heavily wounded Blackbeard across the throat and sailed to Virginia for his reward, with Blackbeard's head suspended from the bowsprit.

43

PIRATES ON TRIAL

Pirate trials were usually short, often lasting no longer than two days. Most experienced pirates, especially those who had used weapons to intimidate their victims, were condemned to death, but younger crew members were sometimes pardoned. Those of any age who had accepted pardons but then returned to piracy were shown no mercy. Executions were carried out in public and immense crowds gathered to watch. At first, all pirates captured by the British had to stand trial in London. In the 1700s, imprisonment, trials and executions were moved to the places where pirates were active, in order to frighten them more. Mass hangings increased, such as 50 of Roberts' company at a castle on the west coast of Africa. Governments hoped that publicity about the fate of captured pirates would deter others. After three tides had washed over them, tarred bodies were displayed in iron cages at places where they would be seen by sailors coming into port. Although piracy continued, it was drastically reduced. The 'Golden Age' of piracy was over.

IN COURT
During the 1700s in the Caribbean, powerful island officials, such as the Governor of Jamaica, presided over the courts. Pirates were charged with attacking and taking ships and boats, stealing cargo, assault and sometimes murder.

Pirates defended themselves as best they could. The two most common defenses they offered were that they had either been forced, on pain of death, to join a pirate crew or had agreed when too drunk to know what they were doing.

44

Pirates were imprisoned at Marshalsea Prison in London, until the 1700s. They were shipped in chains from wherever they had been captured to stand trial. If sentenced to death, they were brought by cart to Execution Dock, at Wapping, on the river Thames.

BARTHOLOMEW PORTUGUES

It was extremely rare for captured pirates to escape. In the 1600s, Bartholomew Portugues, however, was one who succeeded. He made a dramatic last-minute escape from certain execution after he was imprisoned on a ship. Even though he could not swim, he managed to float away to safety, clinging fast to some empty earthenware containers.

FACT AND FICTION
⚓

Mary Read and Anne Bonny were captured when Calico Jack's sloop was attacked by a British naval ship. They were tried in Jamaica in 1720 and all the witnesses at their trial insisted that both women had been fierce and willing pirates. All three pirates were swiftly found guilty and sentenced to death.

Calico Jack was hanged, but only in the final moments of the trial did the two women reveal a secret that saved them from hanging. They were both pregnant. However, Mary Read died of fever in prison before her child was born. The fate of Anne Bonny remains an unsolved mystery.

A priest accompanied a pirate on his last journey from prison to the gallows. As the cart trundled through the waiting crowds, the priest tried to persuade the condemned man to seek forgiveness for his actions. He stood beside the prisoner at the gallows and said a prayer at the moment of death.

Bodies hung in iron cages were coated in tar to protect them from decay, so that they would remain visible for as long as possible. Calico Jack's body was hung in a cage where it could be seen from the main port in Jamaica. Other pirates were displayed along the eastern coast of America and at prominent places on the approach to London along the River Thames. William Kidd's body hung at Tilbury, as a dire warning for several years.

WHO'S WHO

Henry Avery
(1665-1728)
Born near Plymouth, England, Avery was an associate of Thomas Tew and made a huge fortune from piracy. He was last seen in New Providence in the Bahamas.

Aruj Barbarossa
(c. 1474-1518)
Kheir-ed-Din Barbarossa
(died 1546)
These brothers originally came from a Greek family, although they became Muslims. They served in the Turkish navy, before becoming leaders of the Barbary corsairs.

Sam Bellamy
(active c. 1717)
This Englishman became a pirate when he went to North America. He captured a treasure ship, the *Whydah*, but died when it sank off Cape Cod. Its wreck was discovered in 1984.

Anne Bonny
(active 1720)
Born in Cork, Ireland, Bonny's father was a lawyer and her mother a maid-servant. She became Rackham's partner and they attacked Spanish ships off Cuba and Hispaniola. Anne was renowned for her fierce fighting.

Christopher Columbus
(1451-1506)
In 1492, in the employ of King Ferdinand and Queen Isabella of Spain, Columbus landed in the Caribbean, paving the way for the European contact with the Americas.

Stephen Decatur
(1779-1820)
Born in Maryland, North America, Decatur commanded the schooner, *Enterprise*, in battles against Tripoli. He was killed in a duel with a fellow American naval officer.

Sir Francis Drake
(c. 1540-1596)
Born in Devon, England, Drake went to sea at the age of 14. He became an English national hero for his privateering exploits against Spanish ships between 1567 and 1596. In 1581, he was knighted by Queen Elizabeth I, who called him, 'my pirate'.

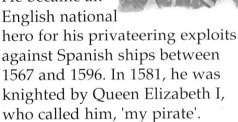

Alexandre Esquemelin
(c. 1645-1707)
A French surgeon-buccaneer who wrote *Bucaniers of America* in 1678, an account of the Tortuga buccaneers.

Sir John Hawkins
(1532-1595)
A Plymouth merchant and slave trader. He died of dysentery and was buried at sea in the Caribbean.

William Kidd
(c. 1645-1701)
Born in Greenock, Scotland, Kidd became a privateer and later took up piracy in the Indian Ocean. He amassed a fortune, some of which he buried.

François le Clerk, 'Jambe de Bois'
(active in the 1550s)
Operated in the Caribbean, attacking Spanish ships off Hispaniola.

Edward Low
(active 1720-1724)
Born in London, he began robbery as a child and his brother was hanged as a thief. He was marooned by his own crew, but managed to escape. His eventual fate is unknown.

Robert Maynard
Commissioned by the Governor of Virginia to hunt down Blackbeard, naval lieutenant Maynard killed him in a fierce fight aboard *HMS Pearl* at Ocracoke Inlet.

Monsieur Misson
Born in Provence, France, into a rich family, Misson was well-educated. He became a sailor because his family had too many children to support. He was a contemporary of Thomas Tew.

Sir Henry Morgan
(c. 1635-1688)

Born in Wales, Sir Henry Morgan sailed to Barbados in his youth. He became an exceedingly successful buccaneer, plundering both Spanish ships and treasure ports. Knighted for his activities, he died of drink after becoming a rich plantation owner.

Chaloner Ogle
(1681-1750)

Ogle was the only naval commander who was knighted for his pirate hunting activities. He became very rich from all the rewards he received.

François Ollonais (Jean-David Nau)
(c. 1620s-1668)

Born in Les Sables d'Olonne, France, Ollonais became one of the most violent and brutal buccaneers.

Bartholomew Portugues
(active 1660s-1670s)

A Portuguese buccaneer based in Jamaica. After his spectacular escape from imprisonment on board ship, Portugues survived by living wild in the forest and building a wooden raft to take him back to his fellow pirates.

Jack Rackham, 'Calico Jack'
(died 1720)

The quartermaster of Charles Vane's ship, who was voted by its crew to become captain in Vane's place. He was unusual in allowing women pirates on board. He was hanged in Jamaica.

Mary Read
(1690-1720)

Born in London, she was brought up as a boy. Later, disguised as a man, she became a footman to a French lady, fought as an army cadet and ran a public house (bar) before becoming a sailor on a merchant ship. When her ship was captured in the Caribbean by Rackham, she joined his crew.

Bartholomew Roberts
(1682-1721)

Born in Wales, Roberts operated as pirate both in the Caribbean and off the west coast of Africa and raided almost 400 ships.

Alexander Selkirk
(1676-1721)

Scottish-born Selkirk was a fisherman before he became a privateer. In 1709, during the voyage of circumnavigation led by Woodes Rogers, he asked to be marooned. He lived alone on the island of Juan Fernandez for over four years before being rescued.

Bartholomew Sharp
(c. 1650-c. 1699)

Born in London, the last known sighting of Sharp was in the Caribbean.

Edward Teach, 'Blackbeard'
(1680?-1718)

Born in Bristol, England, Blackbeard had a short-lived, but notorious, career as a pirate along the North American coast. When he died in battle, he was reputed to have received twenty cutlass slashes and five shots before he finally fell.

Thomas Tew
(active 1684-1695)

Born in Newport, Rhode Island, Tew attacked Moghul ships in the Red Sea and acquired a fortune. He was killed in battle.

Charles Vane
(died 1719)

This pirate captain was ousted from his ship by his crew. He attacked shipping in the Caribbean until he was captured and hanged in Jamaica.

Captain Woodes Rogers
(died 1732)

As a privateer, Woodes Rogers circumnavigated the world between 1708 and 1711. Later, he became a successful pirate hunter.

INDEX

A
Americas *see* Spanish Main; United States
amphorae 8
amputation 34
anchors 22, 23
Anglo-Saxons 9
animals on board 23
Arabs 14
astrolabes 24
attack, methods of 38, 40-1
Avery, Henry 14, 15, 46
axes 9

B
backstaffs 24
Bahamas 12
baldricks 39
ballast 22
Barbarossa brothers 10, 35, 46
Barbary states 10
Bellamy, Sam 25, 45, 46
bilge pumps 26, 27
Blackbeard *see* Teach, Edward
Bonny, Anne 29, 45, 46
booty *see* plunder
boucans 18
boys, ships' 36
brandy 36
Brethren of the Coast 18-19
Britain 10, 16, 42, 43, 44, 45
buccaneers 18-19

C
Cacafuego galleon 17
Caesar, Julius 8
cannons 23, 42
captains 22, 26, 28, 30, 33, 36
Caribbean Sea *see* Spanish Main
carpenters 23, 26, 27, 34, 41
castaways 32
cat o' nine tails 33
catapults 8
caulkers 27
Charles II, King 19, 25, 29
charts, sea 17, 24, 25
cimarrones 17
clothes 19, 28-9
coins 12, 36
Columbus, Christopher 12, 46
compasses 24, 25
compensation, injury 33, 34, 35
cooking 31
coopers 26, 27, 41
corsairs 10-11
cutlasses 33, 38, 39

D
daggers 38, 39
dancing 31
dead reckoning 24
Decatur, Stephen 10, 46
dhows 14
discipline 32-3
doubloons 36
Drake, Sir Francis 17, 46
drink 18, 22, 30, 35
duels 33

E
East Indies 17
Elizabeth I, Queen 16, 17, 46
England *see* Britain
equality 32, 33
executions 44, 45

F
fabrics 15, 28, 29
flags 21
flintlock pistols 38, 39
flogging 32, 33
food 9, 18, 19, 22, 23, 30, 31
France 10

G
galleons 13, 17
galleys 8, 11, 20
gambling 31, 33
gold 36
grain 8
grappling hooks 38
Greeks 8, 33, 46
grenades 38
gunpowder 18, 22, 38

H
hammocks 22
Hands, Israel 39
Hawkins, Sir John 16, 46
helmets, Viking 9
helmsmen 27
Hispaniola 12, 18, 19
Holland 10, 14
household goods 36, 37
hygiene 27, 34, 35

I
illness 34
imprisonment 45
Indian Ocean 14-15, 36
injuries 34-5

J
Jamaica 37, 44, 46
Jefferson, Thomas 11, 47
jewelry 36, 41
Jolly Roger 21

K
keel hauling 32, 33
Kidd, William 20, 35, 37, 45, 46
knots 24

L
lace 28
latitude and longitude 24, 25
le Clerc, François 35, 46
lead lines 24
letters of marque 16
lodestones 24
log and line 24, 25
longships, Viking 9
lookouts 27
loot *see* plunder

M
Madagascar 14, 15, 37
Malta 10
marooning 32, 33
Marshalsea Prison 45
Maynard, Robert 42, 43, 46
medicine chests 34
Misson, Monsieur 21, 46
Moghuls of India 14, 15
monasteries 9
monsoon winds 14
Morgan, Sir Henry 19, 21, 47
music 31, 33
muskets 18, 32, 38

N, O
navigation 17, 24-5
octants 25
Ogle, Chaloner 42, 43, 47
olive oil 8
Ollonais, François 19, 47

P
Panama 17
Philadelphia (US ship) 10, 11
Phoenicians 8
pieces of eight 36
pistols 38, 39
plunder 14, 17, 33, 36-7, 41
Portobello 12, 19, 21
Portugal 14, 16
Portugues, Bartholomew 45, 47
Potosi (Peru) 12, 13
privateers 15, 16-17, 18, 35, 37
punishments 32, 33

Q
quartermasters 26, 31, 33
Quedah Merchant plunder 37

R
Rackham, Calico Jack 21, 26, 29, 42, 45, 47
ratlines 23, 26
Read, Mary 34, 45, 47
Roberts, Bartholomew 20, 21, 28, 31, 32, 33, 42, 43, 47
Robinson Crusoe (Defoe) 32
Rogers, Woodes 42, 47
Romans 8, 46
rules 32-3

S
Sabbath 31, 33
sails 20, 22, 23, 26
sand-glasses 24, 25
schooners 20
scurvy 34
sea chests 31
Selkirk, Alexander 32, 47
Sharp, Bartholomew 25, 47
shields, Viking 9
ship, types of 20
shipwrecks 25
silver 12, 13, 28, 36
skull and crossbones 21
slaves 11, 13, 14, 16, 36
sloops 20
snuff 31, 36
Spain 16, 17, 18, 25, 36
Spanish Main 12-13, 14, 36, 42
Spice Islands (Moluccas) 14, 15
spices 14, 15, 17
steering gear 22, 24, 27
stinkpots 38
surgeons 34, 35, 41
swords 9, 39

T
Teach, Edward 20, 21, 33, 39, 42, 43, 47
Tew, Thomas 14, 15, 21, 35, 37, 47
tobacco 36
Tortuga 18
treasure 12, 17, 36-7
Treasure Island (R.L.Stevenson) 25, 39
trial, pirates on 44-5
Tripoli 10, 11
turtles 19, 30

U, V
United States 10-11, 16
Vane, Charles 26, 42, 47
Vikings 8, 9, 46

W
walking the plank 33
weapons 9, 18, 32, 33, 38-9, 42
wigs 28
windlasses 26
Windward Passage 12
wine 8, 36, 37
women 28, 29, 33, 37

GREENLAND

NORTH
AMERICA

ATLANTIC OCEAN

CENTRAL
AMERICA

Cuba

Hispaniola

Jamaica

Caribbean Sea

PACIFIC OCEAN

SOUTH
AMERICA